Without Rival
the story of the
wonderful
Cave of the Winds

RICHARD RHINEHART

PHOTOGRAPHY BY DAVID HARRIS

The Donning Company/Publishers

184 Business Park Drive, Suite 106

Virginia Beach, VA 23462

Steve Mull, General Manager

Barbara A. Bolton, Project Director

Pam Forrester, Project Research Coordinator

Dawn V. Kofroth, Assistant General Manager

Sally C. Davis, Editor

Lori Wiley, Graphic Designer

John Harrell, Imaging Artist

Library of Congress Cataloging-in-Publication Data

Available upon request

Printed in the United States of America

THE
DONNING COMPANY
PUBLISHERS

Contents

All photographs by David Harris except as noted

Breezeway Cave in Williams Canyon was only discovered by cavers in 1993. However, its remarkable anthodites are considered world-class. Dave Sherrow examines one such display in the Elkhorn Chambers. (Photo by David Harris.)

Introduction
the charm of exploration

In my mind, I can remember my last visit to the chamber as if it was only yesterday. Deep within rugged Temple Mountain in the shadow of famous Pikes Peak, not far from the resort community of Manitou Springs, lies a cherished place called Silent Splendor.

Here, time has almost no meaning and is measured only by the slow drip-drip-drip of droplets of water falling from crystalline white calcite and aragonite. In complete and utter darkness, in a land knowing neither wind nor rain, exquisite crystal minerals leisurely grow over the passing centuries, following blueprints known only to nature.

As guests in this strange land of crystal minerals, we wander in awe, pausing to ponder the origins of these curious creations. Speaking in hushed tones, as if not to awaken the slumbering mountain, we are amazed by the complexity and intricacy of the natural rock features.

Appearing not dissimilar to pearls on a string, these strange beaded helictites crowd Silent Splendor's western wall, competing for our consideration. Brilliant white against the ruddy limestone wall and muddy clay floor, the crystal helictites twist and turn as if gravity had no meaning. Reaching an astounding two feet or more in length, some hang far over the muddy, unforgiving floor as if to taunt the very laws of physics.

With beads ranging from the size of a pinhead to that of a cultured pearl, the helictites appear strangely lifelike, encouraging the wary visitors to apply familiar names to these unfamiliar forms. The sea anemone calls for our undivided attention, while the Mickey Mouse Hand pulls us closer for a more intimate look. The pipe cleaner patiently awaits our incredulous gaze, while other crystal displays seem not unlike the roots of a vegetable garden on the mountain above us.

All too soon our visit must end and our group reluctantly makes its way through the muddy, boot-sucking passage back to the steel ladder leading down into the Whale's Belly. As we pass through the protective environmental gate at the base of the Whale's Belly and into the muddy crawlways stretching to the commercial tour route of the Cave of the Winds, each recalls our utter delight when first seeing Silent Splendor's wonders. In a popular cave that has been visited by literally millions since its discovery over 130 years ago, it is remarkable that such pleasing chambers remain unspoiled and pristine from the eager hand of man. Given that the discovery of Silent Splendor was only in 1984, the question arises how many more of these hidden chambers remain to be found.

Knowledgeable geologists are quick to point out that the mountain in which Cave of the Winds lies has only superficially been examined and probed for hidden corridors and chambers. Since 1982, when members of the National Speleological Society began exploring, surveying, and studying the caves of scenic Williams Canyon, a number of outstanding discoveries have been made both within the Cave of the Winds and in other caves. Although the total passageways in the more than sixty known caves of the canyon now stretch beyond six miles, it is likely that as much or more is as yet unknown. The difficulty lies in determining where these seemingly random passages and chambers await discovery and then opening a passable route.

In April 1993, a group of Denver cavers chanced upon a curious blowing hole in the canyon wall not far from the Cave of the Winds. Over the next six weeks, they worked to enlarge the opening, removing rock, dirt, and other debris. Finally, the windy crawlway lead the cavers beyond a tight jumble of rocks into an immense new chamber they called Cowboy Heaven.

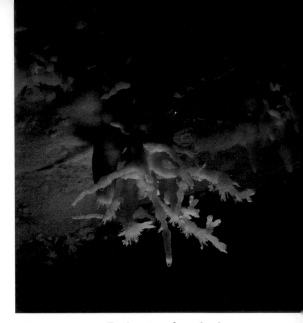

Exploration of new lands brings surprises around every bend in the passage. In Silent Splendor, cavers discovered exquisite aragonite formations unlike anything previously known in the cave. (Photo by David Harris.)

Rivaling the great chambers of the Cave of the Winds, the cave explorers realized this previously unknown room stretching for hundreds of feet in the darkness might someday prove to be the beginning of another great Williams Canyon cave. Today, following persistent exploration, Breezeway Cave has over a mile of surveyed passage and

Digging often reveals hidden passageways, particularly in the clay-filled caves of Williams Canyon. Many of the canyon's most treasured passages were discovered through digs like this one. (Photo by David Harris.)

Top: Cave exploration can be tiring. Here, caver Dave Sherrow climbs a chimney, or crevice, in the Cave of the Winds. (Photo by David Harris.)

Bottom: The spirit of exploration is strong for cavers. Steve Lester pauses in a low passage in Breezeway Cave. (Photo by David Harris.)

exquisite chambers that equal or surpass most anything yet found in its more famous neighbor.

Discovered in 1869, and first opened to public tours in 1880, the Cave of the Winds has welcomed visitors continuously since February 1881. One of the West's first commercially shown caves, the cave's unique location at the top of a mountain at first seems unusual to visitors accustomed to descending into caves from the surface. Yet, owing to the uplift that created Colorado's mighty Rocky Mountains, the cave is now perched on the western rim of Williams Canyon, a 600-foot-deep gorge draining south to Manitou Springs.

It is through this unique geology that the many caves of the canyon developed. Ascending mineral waters that still bubble forth in Manitou Springs today mixed with descending ground water flowing south along the dipping limestone rock. In this mixing zone of two waters, the aggressive water dissolved the soluble rock and created numerous passageways that become blocked with clay, rock, and silt from impurities in the limestone and from streams flowing into the caves.

Stretching the length of the canyon, it is these passageways that cavers actively seek out today. Though the view of craggy Williams Canyon and the Pikes Peak region is stunning, cavers continue to venture underground in search of undiscovered places. Like the generations of explorers of earlier eras who sought out the mountains, valleys, and plains of our surface world, cavers are passionate about discovering new regions below the surface. It's a world of mystery and enchantment, one where the next big discovery might be just around the corner.

For most of the 200,000 annual visitors to the Cave of the Winds, it is exciting enough to tour the commercial tour route that winds through the mountain. While explorers using candles, lanterns, and carbide lamps once cautiously examined these passages, the installation of electric lights in 1907 brings encouragement for those less adventurous.

The adventure is still there—it's just a little more civilized for the modern visitor.

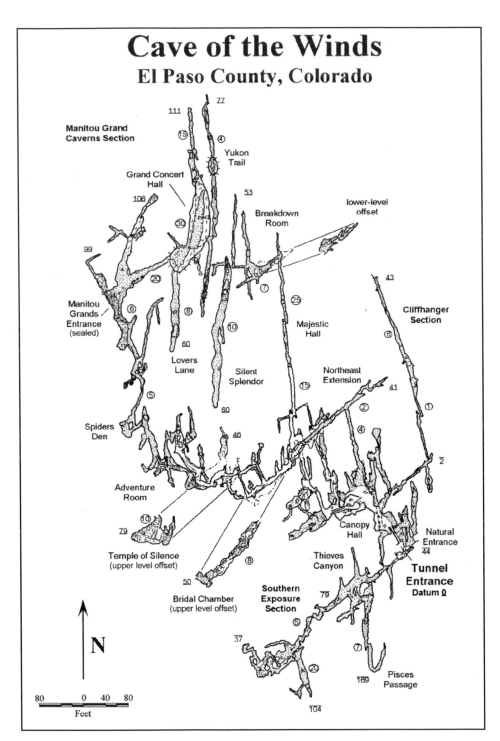

Cave of the Winds
El Paso County, Colorado

Survey map of the Cave of the Winds by the Williams Canyon Project, NSS.
(Map courtesy of Paul Burger.)

Chapter One
visiting the cave of the winds

Perched high on the west rim of scenic Williams Canyon, the entrance building to the Cave of the Winds has a commanding view of Manitou Springs and the Fountain Creek valley stretching far to the southeast. Clinging to the precipitous limestone wall, the entrance building provides a clear view of the floor of Williams Canyon six hundred feet below. There are many small caves visible in the walls of the canyon, though most caves of any length are hidden from view.

Travel to the Cave of the Winds is by the all-weather Serpentine Drive highway, switch backing steeply up from the U.S. Highway 24 Bypass above Manitou. Built in 1915 as the exit route for traffic from the cave, the road was later widened for two-way traffic. It became the sole route after heavy rains in 1995 damaged the historic Williams Canyon road that led through the famous Narrows into Manitou Springs.

From the spacious parking area on the Temple Mountain ridgeline, visitors descend to the Cave of the Winds entrance building. Opened in 1895 with the construction of the cave's entrance tunnel and the ascending Temple Drive from the canyon floor, the building has seen numerous additions and remodeling in the century since. More recently, in 1976, the airy pavilion building was constructed to commemorate the United States' bicentennial and to provide additional visitor space.

At seven thousand feet, Cave of the Winds is one of the highest commercially operated caves in the United States. Nearly 200,000 visitors annually visit the cave and scenic Williams Canyon, which are open to the public throughout the year. For the most part, cave temperatures range from 48 degrees to 54 degrees, so light coats are recommended. Three cave tours are available for the visitor, each offering different underground experiences.

Cave of the Winds Discovery Tour

Following the upper level of the route established in 1881 by original developers George Snider and Charles Rinehart, the Discovery

Visitors are delighted by the spectacular view of Williams Canyon from the Cave of the Winds entrance building. (Photo by David Harris.)

Tour is the most popular tour at the Cave of the Winds. Lasting approximately forty-five minutes, the tour visits about three-quarters of a mile of cave, climbing and descending approximately sixty feet.

Visitors on this tour visit many of the cave's more famous chambers on a paved trail along an electrically lit route. Lights were installed in the cave in 1907, one of the first caves in the United States to use electricity. The great inventor Thomas Edison was fascinated by the underground electrical system in a 1915 visit.

From Curtain Hall just inside the cave's tunnel entrance, visitors are brought into spacious Canopy Hall, one of the larger rooms on the Discovery Tour. This room was discovered by George Snider in January 1881 and encouraged him to partner with fellow Ohioan Charles Rinehart to purchase the cave and open it as an attraction. At one side of this well-decorated chamber, a man-made portal offers a glimpse of the original tourist route descending to the cave's now abandoned lower levels and original entrance. Until the opening of the entrance tunnel in 1895, all tours entered and descended through this dusty portal.

From Canopy Hall, the tour enters the twisting and winding Boston Avenue, so named because it reminded many of the early 1880s touring parties of their Boston hometown streets. Reception Hall is at the far end of the avenue; for many years, visitors were permitted to leave their calling cards on the walls for others to view. A decrepit ladder is seen dangling from a high dome; this was the original route into this room followed by George Snider.

Visitors then climb a steep stairway and enter Manitou Dome, a chamber with several passages branching to different destinations. Many tours follow a passage leading north into Majestic Hall, the longest known single corridor in the Cave of the Winds. Exhibited since the 1880s, this room leads north several hundreds of feet and provides access to the spectacular Silent Splendor.

Both the Discovery Tour of the Cave of the Winds and the historic Lantern Tour of the Manitou Grand Cavern begin at the Visitor Center. (Photo by David Harris.)

Retreating almost back to Manitou Dome, the tour passes by Elmer's Grotto, a shadowy side chamber with a large stalagmite. Turning into another side passage, the visitors enter the once stunning Crystal Palace. When opened to the public in 1885, the Palace was among the most beautiful of all known chambers in the cave. Its ceiling was originally covered with rare "flowering alabaster," what we now call beaded helictites.

Unfortunately, the close proximity of the tour groups to the rare beauties overhead encouraged illegal harvesting of the "flowers," even after protective wire netting was installed. Today, the passage is a sad reminder of how uncaring visitors can devastate a natural wonder.

Continuing into the mountain, the tour passes by several short side passages, each originally filled with beaded helictite displays of exceptional beauty. These rooms were opened for display in 1905.

At a junction in the passage, the tour turns right, into the Old Curiosity Shop. This passage was excavated and opened to the public in 1989, the most recent corridor to be opened along the Discovery Tour. The El Pueblo Boys Ranch provided much of the labor for the excavation, though cavers from the

Williams Canyon Project provided initial design of the new route. Beaded helictites that once filled this passage's ceiling brought forth the name, though sadly most are now missing.

At the far end of the Shop, a steep circular stairway leads up into a ceiling dome. Following this steep ascent, the tour enters the Temple of Silence, added in 1929. A contest to name this exquisitely decorated chamber was held among visitors, with thousands of entries ranging from Heaven's Portal to Snow King's Palace to Marvel Manor to Jack Frost's Workshop. Ultimately, two entries suggested the name Temple of Silence, and the $100 prize was evenly divided. The Temple is the highest chamber along the route and it nearly reaches the surface. Texas Gulch stretches north from this room; it is one of the most active areas along the Discovery Tour.

Descending the staircase, the tour follows the trail deeper into the mountain. At a place called Guide's Rest, a conglomeration of debris indicates the wall of the ancient Manitou Springs, an important source of water for the developing cave. Nearby, a tiny hole in the ceiling provides a glimpse of the Giant's Bleeding Heart, a mass of flowstone and stalactites.

Through a portal, the tour passes through a former pool basin and enters what originally was another cave in between the Cave of the Winds and the Manitou Grand Cavern.

Canopy Hall is the first sizable chamber reached along the Discovery Tour. This room, discovered by George Snider in 1881, is named for its distinctive rock canopies. (Photo by David Harris.)

Tours entering and exiting the Cave of the Winds pass through Canopy Hall. From near the massive Hercules Column, it is possible to see most of the chamber. (Photo by David Harris.)

Discovered in 1893, this Middle Cave was not added to the tour route until 1935. At that time, during the Great Depression, a wealthy businessman provided the funding to commercialize this section of cave. Known as the Valley of Dreams, the gently descending corridor passes by a curious poem on the wall— "Dreams of mountains, As in their sleep, They brood on things eternal." This poem, by nineteenth century author C. A. Higgins, originally appeared in an 1892 visitor booklet on Arizona's Grand Canyon published by the Santa Fe Railroad. Apparently, this poem was a favorite of the businessman, who requested it be placed on the wall of the new passageway.

The Valley of Dreams is splendidly decorated, with flowstone, stalactites, and stalagmites. A side alcove, the Oriental Garden, provides a glimpse of a small reflecting pool called Clyde Lake, named for an early explorer of the cave.

The tour then swings sharply to the left into the Adventure Room, the newest major chamber to be added to the Discovery Tour. Originally a storage room for debris removed from the 1935 Valley of Dreams commercialization, the Adventure Room was excavated in 1988. One of the larger chambers along the tour route, the room also is the gateway to the Manitou Grand Cavern.

Retracing the route to the Temple of Silence junction, the route ducks under a low spot known as Fat Man's Misery. This point was the original end of the Cave of the Winds and held several inches of water in a small pool. In early 1929, Ben Snider pushed through the narrow, wet opening and discovered the passages beyond.

The trail then climbs up the Steel Stairs to the upper level. A sharp right brings the tour to the Bridal Chamber, where over ninety marriages have been held over the last century. The famous cathedral spires are seen at the top of the short

13

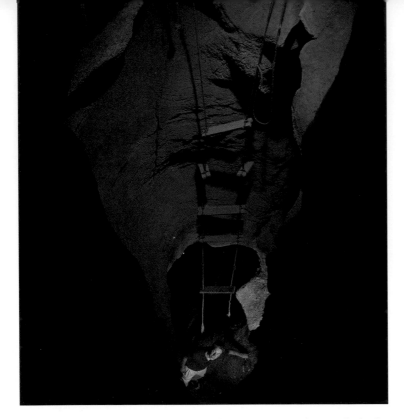

Reception Hall features an apparently ancient rope ladder dropping down from an upper passage. This circular shaft, dropping from the Northeast Extension of the cave's upper level, was the original route into Reception Hall used by explorer George Snider. (Photo by David Harris.)

stairway—for many years, these stalagmites were the symbol of the Cave of the Winds.

Following the upper level back to the northeast, the tour reaches Old Maid's Kitchen, a chamber at the top of Manitou Dome. This chamber contains a large mass of rusting hairpins, many dating back to the early part of the twentieth century. Apparently, in 1910, two women visiting this room declared it to be uninteresting. With approval from the cave's management, they installed a cigar box for unmarried women to place hairpins as a charm for upcoming marriage. Allegedly, the charms worked, as many women later returned to report a successful marriage. Over the years, this mass outgrew the box and was attached to the wall, where it resides to this day.

Descending Manitou Dome, the tour follows the incline of Ordovician Avenue, opened in 1960. This passage ends at another high dome, Zephyr Dome, where a small crawlway leads back into Canopy Hall. Fortunately, the tours are not obligated to follow this historic route and instead use a man-made tunnel to reach the cave's entrance room, which seems much larger after the previous twisting and turning passageways.

Outside, the tour has a glimpse of the cave's original entrance from high balconies overlooking the original archways of the Cave of the Winds, featured in the national *Harper's Weekly* magazine in October 1875.

Grand Cavern Lantern Tour

Cave explorer George Snider opened the Manitou Grand Cavern in 1885. As a competitor to the more-established Cave of the Winds, it attracted more visitors during its twenty-one years of business. Eventually managed by the Cave of the Winds, the Grand Cavern was closed to the public following the 1906 season, when the installation of electric lights in the Cave of the Winds encouraged concentrating visitors along one tour route.

Beginning in 1973 and continuing through the next two decades, "wild" tours for physically fit persons were run into the Grand Cavern through a connecting passageway between the caves opened in 1929. By 1996, these tours were discontinued with the reopening of Manitou Cave in lower Williams Canyon.

Recognizing the need for an adventure tour for families, the Cave of the Winds reopened the Grand Cavern as a lantern tour in 1996. Tours currently enter the system from the Cave of the Winds' Adventure Room. Ascending a tall wooden staircase, the tour gathers kerosene lanterns for their journey into the Grand Cavern.

Discovered by Ben Snider in 1929, the Temple of Silence is the highest chamber along the Discovery Tour. The room is reached by a circular stairway leading from the Old Curiosity Shoppe and Fat Man's Misery. (Photo by David Harris.)

Following the low stooping passages of the Middle Cave to the northwest, the tours travel through the excavated Windy Passage to the end of the nineteenth century commercial route. This passage was excavated in 1929 to allow access to the Grand Cavern, as the cave's entrance tunnel collapsed following heavy rains in the early summer of 1921.

Reaching the historic tour route,

the guide leads the group down a slippery slope beneath the Royal Gorge to the Fairy Bridal Chamber. This nicely decorated room was the scene of several marriages in the nineteenth century, in which the bridesmaids carried torches.

Retreating back to the Rio Grande Tunnel, the tour follows this level dirt-floored route into the large Vestibule, the former entrance chamber of the Grand Cavern. It was this room that George Snider first climbed into from an excavated hole above a large pile of debris. The former entrance tunnel can still be seen, blocked with large boulders.

The Temple of Silence is one of the better-decorated chambers along the Discovery Tour route. One of the more distinctive stalactites is the "Lucky Seven," high above the viewing platform. (Photo by David Harris.)

The main attraction of the room, however, is the silent stone monuments. These pyramid-shaped monuments include the first monument erected in the United States to former President Ulysses Grant following his death in July 1885. Adjacent to Grant's monument are smaller pyramids to President Abraham Lincoln and General Robert E. Lee of the Confederacy. Many of the rocks that form the monuments have the penciled names and initials of the visitors who placed the stones in the late nineteenth century.

Following the Bee Line deeper into the mountain, the Lake Basin is reached. Here, Lover's Lane can be followed to the south to the Butter Churn; to the north is a short passage named Jumbo Tunnel after P. T. Barnum's famous 1880s elephant.

Ducking under a low point, the tour reaches the highlight of the Grand Cavern, the spacious Grand Concert Hall. During the tours of the nineteenth century, Elmore Snider would climb up the steel pipe ladder to the organ loft, where he would play a selection of popular songs on the stalactite organ.

The Concert Hall is one of the larger underground chambers known in Colorado. At its northern end, the Guadalupe Dome reaches far into the darkness above. A large rock wired to the wall is the former Card Rack, where visitors could leave calling cards. Peering over a mound of dirt, a locked gate can be seen—this leads to Snider Hall, a 1982 discovery known for its rare ice crystal impressions on mud walls. Other passageways lead from the southern end of the Concert Hall to discoveries of the 1980s, including Heavenly Hall, the Yukon Trail, Iceland, and Well of Tears.

Returning to the Vestibule, tours sometimes follow Canopy Avenue to a short climb leading to the famous Horseshoe Tunnel. At this climb, a side alcove once held the bones of an American Indian that was discovered in a nearby rock quarry and displayed for several years beginning in 1889.

Grand Cavern tours must follow the excavated Windy Passage back to the Cave of the Winds to return to the surface. Generally, tours take from ninety minutes to two hours or longer and cover well over a mile of cave. Elevation gain is minimal throughout the Grand Cavern—perhaps a few dozen feet at most. Participants must be prepared for dirt and mud floors,

A distinctive feature of the Valley of Dreams is the Pickett Tablet, a rare shield formation. Though common in the caves of New Mexico and Arizona, this is one of only a handful known in Colorado. (Photo by David Harris.)

however, and able to carefully handle lanterns as their only light source throughout the tour.

Manitou Cave Explorer's Tour

In July 1911, local Manitou entrepreneurs D. H. Rupp, T. J. Sandford, and R. D. Weir opened a new competitor to the Cave of the Winds—the New Cave, located along the Williams Canyon road in the lower canyon not far from the resort hotels.

Featuring an electrically lit tour route, an underground lake, a stream, and several sizable chambers and domes, the cave was an immediate success. That first summer, the owners held a contest among tour visitors to name the new cave. Though many names were suggested, Manitou Cave was the winning entry, with the Oklahoma woman offering the name receiving a lot in Manitou's Ouray addition.

Despite the publicity over the naming contest, and the initial interest by curious visitors, decreasing numbers of visitors visited the cave over the next two years. It closed in 1913 and was sold to the Cave of the Winds, who needed the property to construct the new Serpentine Drive road on the ridge above.

Until 1995, the cave lay forgotten and neglected. Canyon floods filled the cave with debris, blocking sections of the former tour route. Amateur visitors mistreated the cave, dumping trash and placing graffiti on its walls. Gating of the cave helped, and in the spring of 1995 the cave reopened for wild tours. Participants for these trips must be physically fit and prepared to squeeze through tight passages, climb rock walls, and bring their own lights. In doing so, they revisit a cave that once was a popular destination, if only for a few years.

Visitors today enter Manitou Cave through a steeply descending passage that once held a stairway. At the

The Oriental Garden was added to the Discovery Tour in 1935. It features long stalactites, columns, and draperies. (Photo by David Harris.)

The Discovery Tour makes a large loop at the Adventure Room, added to the route in 1988. A large wooden stairway in this chamber leads to the Manitou Grand Cavern, once a rival to the Cave of the Winds. Today, costumed guides lead groups with hand-held lanterns into the many chambers of the Grand Cavern. (Photo by David Harris.)

base of the entrance climb, the Whirlpool Dome is found, along with a section of the pipe railing from the early twentieth century tour route.

Through another short climb, the tour follows part of the historic route to the north to a jumbled pile of rock and debris. Here, squeezing through tight excavated crawls, the tour makes its way to the Deepwater Section of the cave. This region, discovered by cavers in 1994, contains several high corridors not on the original tour route.

Returning through the crawlways to the original cave, another section of tour route is followed to the base of the Whirlpool Dome. Here, the visitor has the option of following several crawlways, one leading east into the Centipede Section of the cave. Historic evidence suggests this section had been visited as early as the late nineteenth century, yet it probably was not included on the commercial tour route.

No one knows where the remainder of the former commercial tour route lies in hiding. Many cavers have searched; yet all have been unsuccessful in relocating the reported corridors, chambers, and lake. Participants on the Explorer's Tour are given the opportunity to try their hand at seeking these lost regions during a three-hour visit to the cave.

Other Visitor Tours

During the summer months and on weekends during the winter, depending on the weather, a naturalist leads hiking tours into Williams Canyon and to the ridges and mountains surrounding Cave of the Winds. Tours and activities for children are also regularly scheduled, including educational trips to the undeveloped Snider's Cave north of the historic Manitou Grand Cavern.

At the southern end of Ordovician Avenue, the high Zephyr Dome is found. From the base of this dome, a man-made tunnel leads back to Canopy Hall. Both Ordovician Avenue and Zephyr Dome was added to the tour route in 1960. (Photo by David Harris.)

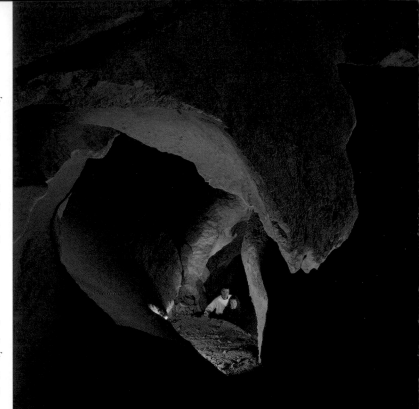

Since the late nineteenth century, numerous weddings have been held in the Cave of the Winds' Bridal Chamber. (Photo by David Harris.)

Grand Cavern Lantern Tours
enter and exit the historic
cavern through this doorway
in the Adventure Room.
Unfortunately, the tunnel
entrance to the Grand Cavern
collapsed after heavy rain in
1921. (Photo by David Harris.)

Tour groups visiting the Grand
Cavern carry hand-held
lanterns to see the passageways
and chambers. When the Cave
of the Winds received electric
lights in 1907, the Grand
Caverns was closed to the public
for the next sixty-five years.
(Photo by David Harris.)

*The Grand Cavern has seen little
change since the last public tours in
1906. Numerous artifacts are found
throughout the cave, including a barrel
of kerosene, old broken lanterns, and a
wheelbarrow. (Photo by David Harris.)*

Manitou Cave is a former commercial cave in lower Williams Canyon. Trips into this cave are limited to visitors who are physically fit and able to crawl through small passageways, free climb rock walls, and even wade through water. (Photo by David Harris.)

Chapter Two
scientific studies in the caves of williams canyon

The charming resort community of Manitou Springs, located at the foot of the mighty Pikes Peak, has been known since the 1870s for its bubbling mineral springs. Naturally carbonated, the spring waters have been a delight for visitors, for both bathing and drinking.

The origin of the spring water lies deep below the city, thousands of feet below the surface. There, water from multiple sources mix in the Ordovician and Mississippian-era limestone strata folded deep along the Ute Pass fault zone.

These waters are exceptionally aggressive in flowing through the limestone, forming caves as they migrate toward the surface. It is from a deep magma body that the water acquires the carbon dioxide that produces the bubbles at the surface. Without the magma, the mineral springs would be decidedly less agreeable to the taste.

Over millennia, as Fountain Creek and other area streams eroded the flanks of Pikes Peak and the Front Range foothills, the springs have migrated along the limestone strata. Over two million years ago, the springs were situated in the former Fountain Creek valley flowing over where the Cave of the Winds is found today. Their colorful mineral deposits can still be seen in the embankment along the cave's upper parking lot.

Speleologists such as Mark Maslyn, Donald Davis, and Dr. Fred Luiszer of the University of Colorado have spent many years studying the geology and hydrology of Williams Canyon. These scientists agree it was the mixing of highly mineralized ascending water and descending ground water from the surface that helped dissolve out the many caves of the canyon. Indeed, careful examination of the walls of Williams Canyon suggests today's caves are but remnants of much more extensive systems that once provided conduits for ancient mineral springs.

With continuing erosion, the caves drained of their mineral waters as the springs sought lower outlets. In the humid, air-filled passages of the caves, leisurely deposits of calcite and aragonite minerals began forming

25

from descending surface water. Over thousands of years, drop by drop, the caves were filled with stalactites, stalagmites, columns, flowstone, beaded helictites, and other speleothems. In many cases, these delicate and fanciful formations took tens of thousands, if not hundreds of thousands, of years to form. Despite study, mineralogists still do not fully understand some speleothems, such as beaded helictites.

Sand, gravel, and clay found within the caves are often the result of streams flowing through the subterranean passageways. Sometimes, clay deposits are also the result of impurities in the limestone, being left behind by slow-moving mineral water.

Cave Life

Despite the high altitude of the caves of Williams Canyon, there is plenty of underground life. Though scientific research is continuing, it is known there are many unique life forms to be identified and studied, some of which is known no where else in the world.

Much of the cave life stays away from the commercial tour trails, instead preferring the quiet and darkness of less visited areas. Places like Thieves' Canyon in the Cave of the Winds have a large variety of thriving insects, living in a unique ecosystem. Though some of these are sightless, many insects travel to the surface on occasion and retain their vision.

Bats are also found in the caves of Williams Canyon. During summer evenings, it is common to see them darting through the night sky, catching and eating flying insects. These flying mammals seldom visit the commercial tour routes, preferring less visited areas in which to sleep during the daylight hours. In recent years, bats have been found in the Cliffhanger and Natural Bridges portions of the Cave of the Winds, as well as in other canyon caves such as Narrows.

Larger animals also use the caves of the canyon as homes or places to sleep. Pack rats are common in most caves, building nests with materials they carry in from outside. In some of the cliff side caves, birds such as falcons make their nests. Away from predators, the caves provide the birds a sense of security as well as a good view. Mountain lions and bears also occasionally use the more obscure caves of the canyon. In the late 1990s, cavers were surprised to come upon a hibernating bear in Pinon View Cave overlooking Manitou Springs.

After the caves drained of water, dripstone, flowstone, and other calcite and aragonite deposits were deposited through dripping water. Here, a group views an impressive bacon strip of calcite in the Temple of Silence. (Photo by David Harris.)

26

Continuing erosion over thousands of years by streams in Williams Canyon and Cavern Gulch intersected the caves, opening cave entrances. Here is a view out of the Cave of the Winds natural entrance looking east across Williams Canyon. (Photo by David Harris.)

With many cave passageways filled with clay and sand, undermining of passages by subsequent water flow can bring about changes. In 1999, heavy spring rains in the Williams Canyon area collapsed a portion of the Temple of Silence floor. Such change is not new in this room, as evidenced by several crooked stalagmites and the Broken Column, shown here. (Photo by David Harris.)

Water continues to enter the Cave of the Winds through natural fissures and cracks in the limestone. In the Valley of Dreams, such a crack is lined by a group of stalactites. (Photo by David Harris.)

Sometimes, the slow drip-drip-drip of stalactites can eventually block passages completely. Fortunately for cavers, this passage, the Manitou Grand Cavern's Horseshoe Tunnel, remains open. It leads to a small, muddy lake. (Photo by David Harris.)

Chapter Three
a century of exploration

High on the west rim of Williams Canyon, overlooking Manitou Springs, the Cave of the Winds welcomes nearly 200,000 visitors of all ages annually. One of the original visitor attractions in the state of Colorado, the cave has been in continuous operation since February 1881. It has seen rivals such as the Manitou Grand Cavern and Manitou Cave flourish and then wither. It has had its share of financial ups and downs, as well as good times lasting decades. Yet, this historic cave continues to attract visitors from across the nation as one of the foremost privately owned and operated show caves in the United States.

One of the early advertisements for the "Wonderful" Cave of the Winds declared it to be "Without Rival." Adding electrical lights that were switched on for the first time on July 4, 1907, the cave boasted, "visitors carry no lantern of any sort," and that the cavern is "perfectly lit" to bring out the wonders of the underground world. Visitors flocked to the cave by railroad and horse and surrey—and later by automobile—climbing to the seven-thousand-foot-high entrance and then descending deep into the mountain. Within the shadow of famous Pikes Peak, the Cave of the Winds had every benefit in becoming a major attraction for Colorado.

Showmanship has always had a role in the history of the cave, from its earliest days under the direction of George Washington Snider. A stonecutter from Ohio who made his way West in 1879 to seek fortune and fame, Snider was perhaps the first promoter of the Pikes Peak region. Discouraged at the lack of big finds in his prospecting efforts and the tedious work he spent as a stonemason on several Colorado railway lines, he spent the winter of 1879–80 examining the curious caves in Williams Canyon, a limestone-walled canyon extending north of the Victorian resort of Manitou.

The trail to the Cave of the Winds. In 1881, the Williams Canyon road ended at the Cave of the Winds building. (Photo from Cave of the Winds collection.)

Early History

Known primarily for its mineral springs, Manitou had long been a popular destination for the Arapahoe, Ute, and other Indian tribes prior

31

to the arrival of the "Pikes Peak or Bust" gold seekers of the 1860s. Though Colorado's territorial capital was at nearby Colorado City, only a few miles to the east along Fountain Creek, Manitou was a lonely place in 1869 when Arthur B. Love settled in Williams Canyon. Taking the canyon with a government homestake claim, Love was primarily interested in the timber for use at his brother's ranch along Monument Creek. Yet, he was intrigued by a peculiar cleft along the canyon's western wall.

Here, a large limestone archway spanned a steep gully extending nearly to the canyon floor. Investigating more closely, he found a dirt-filled cave entrance behind the archway. With plenty of time on his hands, the twenty-five-year-old Love took a shovel and opened up the cave, finding a low, narrow passageway extending into the darkness. With crude pine torches, Love squeezed into his new find, emerging into a large room with

The long stairway. Visitors from 1881 to 1895 followed these wooden stairs up into the Cave of the Winds. The opening of the tunnel portal rendered the stairs obsolete. (Photo from Cave of the Winds collection.)

flowstone cascades and stalactite draperies. Although he realized the cave might have some potential, with the lack of inhabitants or visitors to the region who might pay to see the underground curiosities, he returned to the surface content with his ranching.

Love married in 1874, moving away from Williams Canyon and the Manitou springs. By the following year, Manitou gained several citizens, including James Thurlow, a landscape photographer who documented many of the scenic attractions of the area to earn a living. One of his more popular photographs was a view of this large natural archway, a place he called "The Cave of the Winds" probably after a popular attraction at the famous Niagara Falls near Buffalo, New York. Thurlow's photograph was converted to an engraving for the nationally distributed *Harper's Weekly*, which featured the cave in its October 2, 1875 edition.

Earlier that year, quarrymen working at a small rock quarry for a limestone kiln in lower Williams Canyon found that rocks sent down a steep chute to the Narrows were disappearing into a crack. Curious, the workers opened the natural crevice and discovered a sizable entrance corridor of an unexplored cave that led deep into the mountain. Recognizing the growth of Manitou as a resort would bring visitors to the area, the cave's owners Case and Wilcox decided to commercialize it. Installing ladders and clearing pathways, by early April 1875, Mammoth Cave opened to visitors who eagerly paid an entrance fee of fifty cents.

By the time of Snider's journeys into the canyon in the winter of 1879–80, visitors to Mammoth Cave had slowed to a trickle, despite advertising in area newspapers and encouragement to guests of the several hotels in Manitou. Snider visited the Cave of the Winds on one occasion, examining the small shelter cave at the back yet not venturing further into the darkness.

Discoveries

On June 26, 1880, members of the Boy's Exploring Association and their leader, the Reverend Roselle T. Cross,

The road to the Grand Cavern. George Snider's Manitou Grand Caverns was a popular destination in the late nineteenth century. A carriage road from Rainbow Falls just outside Manitou led up Cavern Gulch to a parking area conveniently located at the cave's tunnel entrance. Circa 1895. (Photo from Cave of the Winds collection.)

arrived in Manitou intent to spend the day exploring Mammoth Cave. Despite the charitable direction of the boys group, Tom Green, the owner of the commercial cave, refused to allow the boys to explore without paying the required admittance fee. "Very well, boys," Cross told his group, "We'll go find our own cave!"

Continuing up the rugged canyon, near the popular Bridal Veil Falls, Cross sent his boys to both canyon walls in search of new caves. John and George Pickett, two young boys who were favorites of Cross, followed the well-worn path to the great Cave of the Winds archway. Under this arch, the boys examined a small shelter cave. Excited at their "find," the boys lit their candles and crawled into the dusty chamber. To one side, a narrow crevice over the dusty dirt piles attracted their attention. Noticing their candles flickered in the wind that blew from the crevice, the boys squeezed into the hole. Pushing aside loose dirt and mouse droppings in the crawlway, the boys emerged after fifteen feet into a standing-sized chamber promising adventure beyond.

Returning to the cave's entrance, they called down to the Reverend Cross, who was gathering together the boys for their journey back to

Colorado Springs. Intrigued at their description of a new cave, Cross guided the group up to the Cave of the Winds. Under the majestic archway in the late afternoon shade, they lit their candles for one final exploration. Cross led the way into the cave, the Picketts and the other boys following close behind.

The wondrous sights they saw that day were forever etched upon their memories. A lofty towering room with cascading flowstone and stalactites convinced them this cave was the finest yet discovered in the canyon. Worried of the damage that might come from common tavern knowledge of the cave, Cross led his boys up and over the ridge to the train station in Manitou. They returned to Colorado Springs without saying a word of their discovery to the citizens of Manitou.

In the weeks and months to come, those in Manitou soon learned of their discovery through articles in the local newspapers. A group of men leased the property in July and commenced to prepare pathways and install ladders. A small keyhole leading to a lower level was opened, providing access to the largest chamber yet found. Interested visitors were led through the cave for $1 apiece. Unfortunately, the ongoing expense of preparing the cave for visitation outweighed the number of paying customers. By late summer 1880, the Cave of the Winds closed.

That autumn, George Snider returned to Manitou to spend the winter. Having worked on railroad construction crews during the summer months, Snider was seeking something to which to occupy his winter. On an icy cold December day, while hunting a deer on the high ridge leading north from Manitou, he spotted a plume of steam billowing from a crevice in the limestone. Suspecting a hidden hot spring, he marked the crevice by tying a red handkerchief on a large juniper tree that grew nearby and continued on his hunt.

A month later, George and a group of friends spent the day hiking in Williams Canyon. Having previously explored the canyon during the previous winter, he was curious about the stories of a new cave behind the Cave of the Winds. Finding the entrance door broken down by hooligans, the group lit candles and entered the former commercial cave. Shamefully, thoughtless visitors had already stolen some of the stalactites and draperies that had delighted the Reverend Cross and his boys exploring group the previous June.

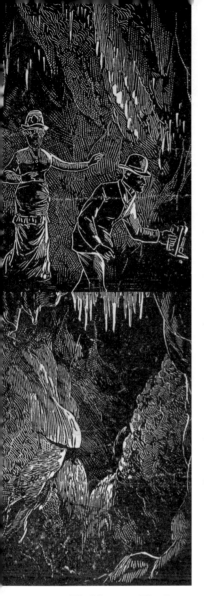

The Narrows; The Grant Monument; The Interior Cascades. Engravings from an 1888 brochure produced by George Snider, proprietor of the Manitou Grand Cavern. (Photo from Cave of the Winds collection.)

From the first large chamber in the cave, a wooden ladder led to an upper level. The explorers followed this ladder, finding the passage ended in large chunks of rock and fill. Setting his candle down for a better look, Snider noticed it flickered noticeably, as if an unseen wind was trying to extinguish its flame. Examining the phenomenon more closely, Snider pulled away a cave rat's nest and found a small opening from which the wind issued.

Tearing down the dirt and rock to see where the hole might lead, debris slumped into it, blocking it completely. With the assistance of his companions, they succeeded in reopening the hole and revealing a small fissure leading into the mountain. Too small to be followed without additional work, they decided to return the following day better equipped to enlarge the passage and follow their new discovery.

Snider returned with Charles Hunter and Charles Rinehart prepared to fully excavate the slender passage. Following several hours of digging, Snider was able to squeeze up and into a new chamber that stretched into blackness beyond the limits of his candle. Snider later recalled, "it was as though Aladdin with his wonderful lamp had effected the magic result" ("How I Found the Cave of the Winds," 1916).

Canopy Hall was the largest chamber yet discovered in the Cave of the Winds and contained exquisite pristine stalactites and stalagmites. Certain its beauty would attract paying visitors, Snider and Rinehart developed a partnership to purchase the cave and reopen it to public exhibition. The owner agreed to sell the eighty acres containing the cave for $1,000, a price the two developers readily accepted.

Over the next month, Snider continued his exploration of his new cave accompanied by his brother Horace. From Canopy Hall, they pushed through dirt and rock chokes into Zephyr and Manitou Domes. At Manitou Dome, they explored to the north, following Majestic Hall to a stalactite and flowstone choke. To the south of the dome, a series of climbs eventually led to the Bridal Chamber and the Cathedral Spires. The explorers also examined many lower-level passages filled with beautiful formations but too small to enter; these later were excavated for the commercial tour route.

Snider hired men to begin preparations of the new commercial tour route. Opening a new tunnel into Canopy Hall

35

from the lower passage, the men installed stairways and cleared trails in the cave. On February 15, 1881, the cave was opened for public tours.

Despite the public interest in the Cave of the Winds, all was not well with the business partnership. Snider quickly discovered Rinehart seemed more concerned in collecting admittance fees from visitors than providing assistance in the development of the cave. Rinehart claimed he was involved with other critical projects for the partnership; "lawyering" Snider later called it. When expenses became due, Rinehart was never around, leaving Snider to cover the costs.

The Grand Cavern

In May 1881, Snider chanced upon the tattered handkerchief he tied to a juniper tree the previous December marking a vapor hole. Investigating more closely, he discovered the hole was steadily drawing air—a sign it led into a cave, not a hot spring as he earlier assumed. With a shovel and pick, he was successful in excavating the crevice, opening a hole leading steeply down into the mountain.

With care, Snider explored this new cave. The new cavern contained remarkable and extensive new chambers, including the Grand Concert Hall, the largest room yet discovered in the caves of the canyon. Developed largely on a single level, Snider decided this new cave might prove more popular than the established cave on the east side of Temple Mountain. Taking a homestead on the property, Snider decided his Manitou Grand Cavern might eventually prove to be a way to escape his unsatisfactory partnership with Rinehart.

In 1884, Snider arranged with his family a trade of his half percentage of the Cave of the Winds for forty acres of land near the Grand Cavern. Knowing the difficulties he had in his previous business partnership with Rinehart, Snider was determined to establish the Grand Cavern as a unique entity that he fully owned. He wanted no confusion over the ownership or management, nor did he want any of the debts of the Cave of the Winds.

Brilliantly illuminated. By 1907, the Cave of the Winds boasted an electric lighting system that relieved visitors of the trouble of carrying lamps to illuminate the passageways. Here two visitors prepare for departure back to Manitou, while other visitors lounge on the porch. (Photo from Cave of the Winds collection.)

For some time, George worked to clear pathways in his new cave. He hired a force of men to build a carriage road to the cave up Cavern Gulch from Rainbow Falls. Finally, in March 1885, the Grand Cavern opened with considerable publicity. It was an immediate success, even though the new tunnel entrance was not yet complete and visitors still had to climb a steep trail from the end of the road.

Through political connections he developed while serving on the Manitou City Council, Snider successfully lobbied the Colorado State Legislature to pass an Act protecting Colorado caves from vandalism. This 1885 Act was the first cave protection law passed in the United States and was successfully used in prosecution at least twice in the next century.

With public attention high on his new cave, Snider also succeeded in passing the rival Cave of the Winds in the number of paid admissions. The morning following the death of President Ulysses Grant in July 1885, Snider encouraged visitors to place stones on a monument to the famous Civil War general. This "monument within a mountain" was the first in the nation to Grant and generated much publicity. In the following years, similar monuments for President Abraham Lincoln and General Robert E. Lee of the Confederacy joined the solemn pyramid of stones. Generals George McClellan and William Sherman placed their stones upon the Grant monument by 1889, with visitors in Sherman's tour group pausing to build a monument to him. Irritated at the gesture, he kicked the stones over, declaring, "I'm not dead yet."

Canopy Avenue leading north from the monuments presented a curious sight for visitors in the late 1880s and early 1890s: the bones of an Indian that were found buried at the Snider sandstone quarry in nearby Red Rock Canyon. The bones were removed by the turn of

the century, presumably properly buried somewhere outside the cave.

The highlight of the Grand Cavern tour was a concert presented on the Grand Concert Hall's stalactite organ. George's younger brother Elmore became skilled at playing the stalactites, and mastered popular tunes such as "Rousseau's Dream" and "God Save the Queen" to the delight of the visitors. On occasion, other musicians or vocalists would accompany his playing.

The Grand Cavern even had a Fairy Bridal Chamber, where on occasion a couple would join in marriage. The bridesmaids carried torches to light the procession and Elmore would play the wedding march on the Concert Hall organ.

Lawsuits and the Joining of the Caverns

With all the attention Snider's Grand Cavern was receiving following its opening, the management at the Cave of the Winds was undoubtedly concerned. Although they opened the fabulous Crystal Palace with its beaded helictites to tours in 1885, revenues lagged far behind the newly popular cave across the mountain.

On October 1, 1886, Rinehart's wife Rose filed in local court for half interest in the Grand Cavern, stating that portions of the cave lay on Cave of the Winds property. Though Snider had long since traded his interest in the Cave of the Winds for additional property, the Rineharts believed the agreement still applied. Any business operations on the original property were to be shared equally.

Over the next decade, various suits and counter suits were filed between the parties. While the original trial ended in favor of Snider with a confirmation that the Grand Cavern lay entirely on his property, new surveys commissioned by the

The Bridal Chamber. One of the more spectacular rooms on the Cave of the Winds tour was the Bridal Chamber. This chamber was well known for its Cathedral Spires, the stalagmites to the left, and Dante's Inferno, a group of helictites to the right (out of sight). (Photo from Cave of the Winds collection.)

George's discovery. This view of the famous Canopy Hall, presumably dating from about 1907, shows the cave had yet to gain the luxury of paved trails. Note the electric wiring for lights draped over the rock to the left. (Photo from Cave of the Winds collection.)

Rineharts showed the cave extended beneath their property. A second trial at district court with the new surveys ended in favor of the Rineharts in 1888, requiring Snider to pay them half the revenues since the Grand Cavern's opening.

Snider attempted to appeal the case to the Colorado Supreme Court in 1889 and again in 1892. Unfortunately, owing to a filing error and the subsequent deaths of both Rineharts, the Supreme Court declined to consider the case, even though they admitted it seemed worthy of their consideration.

In January 1895, the Supreme Court confirmed the decision of the lower court and ordered Snider to provide the Rinehart estate with half interest in the Grand Cavern. Though Snider's attorneys attempted to appeal to Federal courts and delayed the official transfer, by 1899, Rinehart's daughter Emma Austin sued to satisfy earlier judgments in her favor. She asked that the Grand Cavern operations be formally transferred to the Cave of the Winds and that $10,000 be paid to her for back revenues. The court agreed and the Grand Cavern was given to the Cave of the Winds. George Snider had moved to California by that time, seeking new business ventures. He sold his half interest in the Cavern in 1916 and died in California on June 26, 1921—forty years to the day of the Pickett brother's discovery of inner Cave of the Winds.

With both caves operated under a common management, George's brother Perry and Charles Austin made business decisions affecting their future. In 1895, the Cave of the Winds built the Temple Drive carriage road from the floor of Williams Canyon to a new tunnel

Temple Drive. In 1895, a force of men carved a road from the floor of Williams Canyon up Temple Mountain to the new tunnel entrance to the Cave of the Winds. This road, shown here in the 1920s, was open to travel until 1995, when heavy spring rains washed out sections of the road. (Photo from Cave of the Winds collection.)

Cave of the Winds brochure. This booklet was distributed in the early 1920s, prior to the discovery of the Temple of Silence. By then, horses and carriages had disappeared and automobiles ruled the roads. (Photo from Cave of the Winds collection.)

entrance leading directly into Canopy Hall. A cliff side entrance building was constructed, with a small gift shop opened by 1896.

Although tours continued through both caves, the management decided they could afford to install electric lights only in the Cave of the Winds. On July 4, 1907, the switch was flipped to illuminate the Cave of the Winds to the approval of the gathered crowd. The Grand Cavern, however, was not opened in 1907. While management claimed the cave would be later reopened for tours with electric lighting, it lay forgotten for many years. By 1921, continued vandalism of the Grand Cavern's entrance building encouraged the Cave of the Winds to dismantle it. The entrance tunnel, refurbished in 1906, was broken into numerous times by vandals until heavy rain in 1921 caused a massive collapse of the wooden tunnel shoring. The cave would not reopen for public tours for a half century.

The Celestial City. In 1929, Ben Snider discovered the "New Room," a magnificent upper-level chamber. The room was named the Temple of Silence in a contest that received thousands of entries. (Photo from Cave of the Winds collection.)

Reorganization, Connections and New Discoveries

The 1911 development of the rival Manitou Cave in lower Williams Canyon and the growing popularity of the automobile forced the Cave of the Winds to seek reorganization as a corporation in 1914.

Dreams of Mountains. The Valley of Dreams was opened by the Cave of the Winds in 1935. Along the wall, a poem originally written by Charles A. Higgins in 1892 for Arizona's Grand Canyon reads "Dreams of mountains, As in their sleep, They brood on things eternal." (Photo from Cave of the Winds collection.)

Oriental Garden. One of the most beautiful chambers in the Cave of the Winds is the Oriental Garden. Opened in 1935, the chamber was originally called "Wonderland." The long stalactite to the left is unbroken in this early 1950s image; careless workers later broke it twice. (Photo from Cave of the Winds collection.)

The recapitalization was necessary to pay debts associated with the October 1913 purchase of Manitou Cave and sixty-five acres of land along the ridge south of the Cave of the Winds. In addition, owing to the narrowness of the Williams Canyon road, the cave management decided to spend $8,000 in constructing the new Canyon Rim Road from the cave to Manitou. Switchbacking steeply down the mountain into Manitou, the new road quickly became known as Serpentine Drive. Its opening in July 1915 allowed automobiles a one-way loop in visiting the cave.

The collapse of the Grand Caverns entrance tunnel in 1921 encouraged the connection underground of the closed commercial cave to the Cave of the Winds. In between the caves was a small, highly decorated cave discovered in 1893. Known as the Middle Cave, Ben Snider and Guy Boyd worked to connect this cave to the larger caves on either side.

In early 1929, Snider squeezed through a low pool at the end of the Cave of the Winds tour route. This "rat hole" as they called it immediately opened into a larger passage. At its far end, a crevice led up into a breathtaking new chamber with many decorations. Commercializing the new section of caves for tours, the Cave of the Winds held a contest that summer to determine a name for the new room. Over 25,000 names were submitted, with two persons suggesting the Temple of Silence.

Snider was not complete with his exploration. Poking through a muddle of rocks that blocked the passage beyond the new chamber, he found a connection into the Middle Cave. Near that cave's entrance, Snider and others excavated a low, windy passage that allowed access into the closed Grand Cavern. Finally, the caves were connected into one system.

Owing to the Depression, it was not until

1935 that funding could be arranged to commercialize a portion of the Middle Cave. This passage, called the Valley of Dreams, was opened with the assistance of a private individual. As a part of the funding, a line from a favorite poem was placed on a wall: "Dreams of mountains, As in their sleep, They brood on things eternal." This poem is from the 1892 "Grand Canyon of the Colorado River" book by Charles A. Higgins regarding Arizona's Grand Canyon.

In 1958, a group of Colorado businessmen approached the Cave of the Winds Scenic Attractions Company to purchase the famous attraction. Though a purchase price could not be reached, the company agreed to a ninety-nine-year lease.

The new management arranged improvements to the cave, including opening Ordovician Avenue and Zephyr Dome in 1960. On the surface, Serpentine Drive was widened and improved for two-way traffic and a large parking lot on the ridge was constructed. For the nation's bicentennial in 1976, the owners added a large addition to the cave's entrance building.

The Grand Cavern was reopened in 1973 on a limited basis for wild caving tours. This arrangement lasted until 1996, when the caving tours were moved to Manitou Cave and lantern tours introduced. New chambers and passageways were also added to the Cave of the Winds commercial tour route in the 1980s. In 1988, a chamber in the former Middle Cave was excavated and named the Adventure Room. The following year, the

The Stalactite Organ. Visitors to the Grand Caverns thrilled to Elmore Snider's playing of the stalactite organ in the Grand Concert Hall. Though today the 1893 ladder is considered unsafe, in 1951, Cave of the Winds traffic manager Guy Boyd (top) and photographer's assistant Cloyd Brunson (bottom) climbed to the loft. (Photo from Cave of the Winds collection.)

Relics. For many decades, relics of the earlier commercial era survived in the Manitou Grand Cavern forgotten and untouched. Here, Cloyd Brunson (left) and Guy Boyd (right) examine an old kerosene lantern found broken and abandoned near the Horseshoe Tunnel in 1951. (Photo from Cave of the Winds collection.)

Old Curiosity Shoppe was opened, allowing an alternate route to Fat Man's Misery—the former pool Ben Snider squeezed through in 1929 in his discovery of the Temple of Silence.

Splendid Discoveries

Cave of the Winds General Manager Grant Carey understood the benefits of allowing volunteer cavers onto his property. Though traditionally the caves of Williams Canyon were closed to all visitors, he believed cavers could help discover new passageways and chambers, as well as help him better understand his cave resources. Since 1978, cavers had provided assistance in controlling access to Huccacove Cave in the lower canyon. In 1982, Carey permitted cavers access to the Cave of the Winds.

The National Speleological Society is this nation's largest and oldest national association for the study, exploration, and conservation of caves. With several chapters in Colorado, the organization was eager to begin work in the Cave of the Winds.

Under the direction of Mark Maslyn, cavers began both a survey project and a dig project in the cave in 1982. The sur-

The modern era. By the 1950s, the Cave of the Winds had enlarged and paved its parking lot for the large automobiles of the era. Tours still cost a dollar, though, a bargain for the time. (Photo from Cave of the Winds collection.)

In Pikes Peak's shadow. Though the top of the famous 14,000-foot peak is not visible from the Cave of the Winds entrance, it can be seen from across Williams Canyon. This view, from the early 1960s, shows the new upper parking lot ready for any overflow parking. (Photo from Cave of the Winds collection.)

vey, the first of two over the next two decades, helped establish the true extent of the system for the first time. The dig, off of the Bridal Chamber, only provided another connection to the passages beyond Fat Man's Misery. However, the Bridal Chamber dig provided the groundwork for dozens of dig projects in the years to follow.

Owing to area geology, many of the passageways in the caves of Williams Canyon contain significant amounts of clay, sand, and gravel. By excavating these natural blockages in the caves, new discoveries are often the result.

In October 1982, cavers successfully opened a previously unknown chamber to the north of the Grand Concert Hall. Named Snider Hall after developer George Snider, the eighty-foot-long room is best known for its curious ice crystal impressions on mud coating the chamber's walls. Scientists believe these impressions may date from the last Ice Age.

One of the most significant discoveries in recent years occurred in January 1984. Following months of excavating sticky clay from lower-level passageways leading west from the Breakdown Room, cavers emerged into the Whale's Belly, a large decorated chamber. A technical rock climb up a sheer wall of this chamber led into Silent Splendor, a stunning passage filled with exquisite white beaded helictites. Containing the best examples of these rare helictites yet discovered, Silent Splendor was the subject of a 1986 television documentary broadcast nationwide on the Public Broadcasting System. Though other displays have since been found in nearby Breezeway Cave that exceeds the beauty of Silent Splendor, the passage is still a favorite destination of cavers.

Looking up from below. Though early tours to the Cave of the Winds entered and exited through the natural entrance, tours since 1895 have used a tunnel entrance providing easier access. Few visitors today enjoy the view from the sinkhole up to the visitor center. (Photo by David Harris.)

Other discoveries followed. In 1986, cavers discovered the Cliffhanger Section of the Cave of the Winds, the longest single new section of the cave found since the discovery of the Middle Cave in 1893. Another short dig opened Natural Bridges Hall, a chamber with seven natural bridges of various lengths that was apparently purposefully sealed many years before.

In the Grand Cavern, digging in a crawlway leading east of the Concert Hall opened Heavenly Hall and the Yukon Trail

in 1989. The former contains a spectacular display of beaded helictites, the latter a beautiful dripstone chamber known as Iceland.

In the lower cave, off of Thieves' Canyon, cavers in 1992 pushed through a jumble of broken boulders. They discovered an extensive area of muddy passages to the southeast, including Southern Exposure and the Valley of the Shadows. This region still has promise of additional discoveries.

More recently, in the spring of 2000, cavers opened a tight squeeze at the northern end of Majestic Hall. This awkward hole immediately led into a three-hundred-foot-long extension, including canyon passage up to

Silent Splendor. Cavers in 1984 dug up into the most treasured room in the Cave of the Winds, Silent Splendor. Though not particularly lengthy, the two-hundred-foot-long passage includes spectacular formations like these. (Photo by David Harris.)

The Brush Cleaner. Silent Splendor includes numerous dazzling sights, including the brush cleaner. This soda straw and the other formations in Silent Splendor are still growing, though exceptionally slowly. (Photo by David Harris.)

sixty feet in height. It is likely this passage will lead further north along the ridge through additional excavation.

With close to eleven thousand feet of surveyed passage, the Cave of the Winds is one of the longest caves currently known in Colorado. Through the continued exploration and study by the Williams Canyon Project, it is likely the cave will continue to grow, with many new remarkable and magnificent discoveries to come in upcoming years.

Williams Canyon is known to have over sixty caves and cave features. Excepting tour groups visiting Manitou and Snider's Caves, the public is not allowed into any of these caves. (Photo by David Harris.)

Chapter Four
a canyon of caverns

Visitors to the Cave of the Winds are often curious if there are other caves in Williams Canyon. Although the Cave of the Winds is the longest and best known of the caves, Williams Canyon and Cavern Gulch have over sixty other known caves and cave features.

Manitou Cave in lower Williams Canyon and Snider's Cave in Cavern Gulch are the only other caves currently open to public visitation. Manitou Cave offers visitors an undeveloped cave experience, following part of the former 1911 commercial tour route as well as visiting the recently discovered Deepwater Section. Snider's Cave is a featured destination for children's activity programs, though these groups venture only a short distance into the cave.

For over twenty years, cavers from the National Speleological Society's Williams Canyon Project have explored, surveyed, and studied the many canyon caves. The great majority of these undeveloped caves are short and uninteresting, averaging only one hundred to two hundred feet in length. Owing to safety considerations, the public is not permitted in any of these caves.

The larger and more interesting caves of Williams Canyon are securely gated, with access restricted to experienced cavers and speleologists participating on trips approved by the Cave of the Winds and the Williams Canyon Project. Experienced individuals interested in joining this volunteer project should contact the National Speleological Society or the Cave of the Winds for additional information.

Manitou Cave

For most of the twentieth century, Manitou was a forgotten, neglected cave. Few knew or cared that it once was a commercially shown attraction that briefly rivaled the Cave of the Winds.

In July 1911, Manitou welcomed its newest visitor attraction: the "New Cave" in lower Williams Canyon, only a few minutes walk from the growing resort community. Three area entrepreneurs, R. D. Weir,

J. F. Sandford, and D. H. Rupp, opened the attraction to a flurry of newspaper publicity, promising a prize for the visitor who could provide the cave a suitable name.

Installing stairs, railings, and electrical lights along the new visitor trail, the partners welcomed visitors who chose not to continue up Williams Canyon to the more famous Cave of the Winds. Through political connections, they were able to convince the city council of Manitou to allow automobiles as far as their parking lot, a privilege denied the Cave of the Winds.

The cave tour included a "spirit lake" where the water level raised and fell mysteriously through the day, a lofty "Whirlpool Dome" and a mammoth "Convention Hall." Published reports of the era told of exceptional potential for new discoveries while offering surprise that such an interesting natural attraction should be located so close to the city. In the autumn of 1911, an Oklahoma woman won the naming contest, receiving a lot in the Ouray addition of Manitou as a prize.

All was not well, however, with Manitou Cave. Less than a year after opening the attraction, the partners leased the cave to John Martin, a local businessman who ran the cave in 1912 and 1913. Vandals attacked the cave in November 1912, stealing all the precious electric light bulbs from the visitor trail.

Financially, the operation was on shaky ground for its final season. Advertising was non-existent and area visitors ignored the operation on their journey up Williams Canyon. In October 1913, the three partners sold the property and the cave to Charles Austin, the majority owner of the Cave of the Winds. He promptly closed down the operation for good.

Over the next seven years, the Cave of the Winds allowed the popular Chief Manitou, a Santa Clara Indian from New Mexico who danced at area attractions, to live at the closed entrance building during the summer months. During this period, Chief Manitou—whose legal name was Pedro Cajeta— allowed visitors the opportunity to explore the closed commercial cave on their own. This arrangement ended in 1921, when heavy rains and a large flood in Williams Canyon washed away the entrance building. The flood also apparently filled Manitou Cave with muddy stream water, filling passages along the former commercial route with road base and other debris.

Though over the next quarter century the Cave of the Winds attempted to keep visitors out of their former rival by

Visitors to Manitou Cave follow a portion of a former commercial route. Open to public tours from 1911–1913, Manitou Cave was purchased by the Cave of the Winds and closed. At the Whirlpool Dome, pipe railings are a reminder of the former tours. (Photo by David Harris.)

cementing and blasting the entrance, determined individuals continued to keep the entrance open. By the 1970s and 1980s, the former Manitou Cave was all but ignored by the Cave of the Winds and cavers, filled with trash and marred with graffiti.

Historical research into the caves of the canyon in the late 1980s renewed interest in the cave. Cavers excavated a debris-choked crawlway under the floor of Williams Canyon in 1988, revealing the forgotten Centipede Cave. This small cave was originally explored in the 1890s and was closed by Manitou authorities in 1908 after a party of visitors from Kansas became lost in the cave with no light. Clearly, Rupp, Sandford, and Weir had connected this obscure cave into their new attraction only a few years after the city closed it as being "unsafe."

With the rediscovery of Centipede, the Cave of the Winds decided to securely gate Manitou Cave in 1993. Shortly thereafter, in February 1994, Jon Barker and Charles Lindscy discovered Deepwater Cave, a previously unknown cave just to the west of Manitou Cave. Following a short connection dig, the entrance to Deepwater Cave was sealed.

From only 700 feet in 1988, the Manitou Cave system expanded to 2,300 feet of passage by 1994. Seeking a new location for their primitive caving tour, the Cave of the Winds decided to reopen the cave in early 1995. Marc "Caveman" Hament developed the cave for tours, adding limited improvements for safety and clearing trails where necessary. Tour groups were encouraged to help in the search for the "Lost Tour," even providing assistance in ongoing digs in the cave.

Manitou's lost tour route remains in hiding, despite the best efforts of both tour groups and cavers. Perhaps someday cavers will once again discover the forgotten regions of the cave, unseen by paying customers since the era of the great luxury liner *Titanic*.

Huccacove Cave

Although the Cave of the Winds has been shown to the public continuously since 1881, the honor of being the first commercial cave in Colorado goes to another Williams Canyon cave.

In March 1875, workers quarrying limestone for the Case and Wilcox limekiln discovered a hidden crevice led into an extensive cave. With an eye toward attracting the increasing number of visitors vacationing at the Cliff House and other hotels in nearby Manitou, the kiln owners installed stairways, ladders, and other improvements.

Tours into the new Mammoth Cave were primitive— for an entrance fee of fifty cents per person, visitors were allowed to tour the nearly one thousand feet of passage so far explored and opened. If a party of six or more approached, suitable clothing, lights, and a guide at no extra charge were provided by the proprietors.

Within a year, Case and Wilcox sold their attraction to Tom Green, who continued as owner until at least 1880. Visitors became increasingly rare through the years and apparently ceased altogether following the discovery of the inner Cave of the Winds by the Pickett boys and the Reverend R. T. Cross. Not only was the Cave of the Winds more attractive, but also the passages were larger and more spectacular. By 1881, when George Snider and Charles Rinehart opened the Cave of the Winds to the public, Mammoth Cave had closed.

Despite its history as Colorado's first underground attraction, Mammoth Cave quickly became forgotten except among school children and adventurers. On September 11, 1891, tourist Charles Duncan of Iowa decided to explore the cave on his own. Exploring the abandoned "Tom Green" cave, Duncan apparently fell down one of the twenty-foot-deep pits connecting the upper and lower levels. His kerosene lantern broken by his fall, he feared he might never make his way to daylight again. In the darkness of the cave, he scribbled his will on the back of an envelope, and then began feeling his way along the passageways on hands and knees. Meanwhile, Grand Cavern

Much of Manitou Cave has never been opened to the public. The Deepwater Section, discovered by cavers in 1994, contains large corridors and tight, sand-filled crawlways. (Photo by David Harris.)

proprietor George Snider led a search party organized by the missing man's hotel. Making their way up the gully to the cave entrance, they came upon Duncan on his way down, successful in his lightless search for the entrance. However, they noted the knees to his pant legs were completely worn through by his crawling.

Despite the dangers with the old cave, it continued to attract visitors. By the early 1910s, the cave received a new name. Although originally shown as Mammoth Cave, local visitors began calling it Hucacode Cave. This curious name comes from combining the first two letters of two couples who explored the cave in the early part of the twentieth century—Hugh, Carl, Cora, and Delia. Why the cave was renamed is a mystery, as is the full identity of the two couples.

Hucacode Cave continued to trouble the owning Cave of the Winds over the next seventy years. In 1916, two young boys exploring the cave by candlelight came upon the body of a twenty-three-year-old man at the foot of Angel Falls, the first large pit along the former commercial route. Investigating police discovered the man had committed suicide by taking cyanide.

Increasingly worried about accidents and injuries in the cave, the Cave of the Winds dynamited the entrance shut several times. Unfortunately, visitors would promptly re-excavate it. Even a concrete cap placed in 1949 failed to deter visitors, who broke the cave open again.

The Colorado Grotto of the National Speleological Society first visited the cave in 1951. Exploring the dusty passageways, the cavers found little of interest. The first map of the cave was completed in 1953, titled "Huccacove Cave" rather than Hucacode. This apparent error by the surveyors changed the cave's name once again to that which is used to this day.

Traffic by amateur explorers grew during the 1950s and

1960s. In the mid-1950s, a group of teenage Colorado Springs boys were lost in the cave for twenty-six hours when their single flashlight burned out. Like the Iowa visitor in 1891, they eventually made their way back to the surface by touch alone.

During the 1960s, it is reported two people on unrelated trips fell to their deaths on the twenty-five-foot Angel Falls climb—making Huccacove the deadliest cave in Colorado history. Other less serious accidents occurred into the 1970s as visitors continued to use the cave for parties. Finally, in 1979, the cave was gated and locked to prevent future unauthorized visits. Though unhappy locals repeatedly vandalized the gate in a misguided effort to maintain free access, by 1987 a strengthened steel gate provided Huccacove full protection.

Since then, cavers have cleaned Huccacove of the trash and graffiti that once filled its passageways. Filling a multitude of trash bags, the cave slowly began to resemble the attraction that Case and Wilcox first opened a century before.

In January 1990, cavers successfully completed a dig through rubble at Huccacove's Blowing Chimney. They discovered thousands of feet of new passageway beyond in what became known as the Mammoth Extension.

This new region of corridors, chambers, and canyons includes passages more like Cave of the Winds than historic Huccacove. Through the Hub, the Aurora Room and Huccy's Secret, cavers came into the spacious God's Country, one of the more spectacular rooms of Williams Canyon. For cavers accustomed to the dusty passages of the historic cave, God's Country with its towering piles of large boulders and delicate calcite formations was like stepping into another cave.

There is promise of additional passageways yet to be discovered in Huccacove. In the years since the discovery of God's Country in the Mammoth Extension, cavers have excavated a number of clay and rock-choked passages. Though nothing spectacular has yet been found, the possibility of another exciting discovery still exists beyond the next shovel of dirt.

Narrows Cave

Colorado cavers are a patient group. While prompt discoveries do happen on occasion, it is more common to spend weeks, months, and even years digging before a new section is opened.

Breezeway Cave was discovered by cavers in 1993. It is the second-longest cave known in Williams Canyon with nearly seven thousand feet of passage. Here, caver Steve Lester traverses through the C Survey Corridor. (Photo by David Harris.)

Consider the story of Narrows Cave. Originally a shelter cave with less than ten feet of passage, it today has nearly a mile of known passage, thanks to the patient digging of Colorado cavers.

In the spring of 1983, cavers decided to excavate an obvious filled cave passage in lower Williams Canyon. Excavation was not easy—the passage had apparently once pirated the Williams Canyon stream and filled with sand and gravel as a result.

Geologists speculated the cave had good potential. Certainly, the stream apparently flowed into it for years without backing up. Only through flood episodes did the cave become overwhelmed with debris, forcing the stream to find another route down the canyon.

During the years of excavation, cavers used a variety of

techniques to follow the passage deeper into the mountain. Folding shovels and hands and knees crawlways gave way to full size shovels, walking sized passage, and wheelbarrows. An electric generator helped the excavation effort, as electric hammers and shovels helped break apart the ancient sand and gravel.

As the months turned into years, cavers continued down the entrance passage, optimistically named Zephyr Avenue in hope of finding an elusive wind that could lead to open passage. On occasion, as the number of participants dwindled, the project would cease until others took up the cause. A large steel chute was constructed to handle dumping of sand and gravel from the cave's entrance. This allowed a dump truck to be placed under the chute to collect the material for use as road base elsewhere on Cave of the Winds property.

By February 1995, cavers had progressed approximately 240 feet into the cave—every foot of it excavated by hand. At this point, an ascending sand-filled tube was found. Digging upward, the cavers excitedly broke into air-filled passage. Naming the climb the Inquisition Dome, the new section at the top was not particularly long or interesting. However, it was the first part of Narrows Cave that did not need excavation.

Returning to the Zephyr Avenue dig, the reenergized cavers continued their efforts along the former stream course. Using a multitude of wheelbarrows to transport the fill to the waiting chute, cavers extended the passage another 140 feet. Here, a sand-filled tube leading upward provided yet another opportunity to rise above the sand and gravel fill. In April 1996, cavers triumphantly entered new passage at the top of the Resurrection Dome.

This new section was unlike the earlier discovery at the top of the Inquisition Dome. Larger and more complex, the cave seemed willing to allow cavers a break from years of digging.

To reach the passages beyond Holy Waters, cavers like Bill Allen had to traverse sock or bare-footed along a narrow ledge. Concerned with the impact of cavers on the delicate cave environment, a bridge eventually was constructed that today spans the pool. (Photo by David Harris.)

Indeed, this upper level passage proved to be the key in opening up the cave.

From the top of the Resurrection Dome, cavers followed Shakedown Street to the Moonglow Room. Another high dome, called Idiot's Paradise, led forty feet to an upper level of large echoing passageways. Explored in July 1996, this new level proved to be the most impressive yet in Narrows Cave. The large rooms—Zig-Zag Canyon, Leavenworth, the Boulder Buick Room, and Alcatraz—are among the most spacious in any Williams Canyon cave.

Other passages led to a complex series of crawlways, squeezes, and climbs. From the Moonglow Room, cavers dug and squeezed their way into the Subluna Passage, Spring Canyon, and Southern Scoops. Surveyors followed far behind the explorers during the late 1990s, as new discoveries were made nearly every week.

By the end of the twentieth century, Narrows Cave had taken its place as one of the major caves of Williams Canyon. Strong wind in the cave suggests there is probably much more yet to be found.

Breezeway Cave

Generations have searched the walls of Williams Canyon for fame, fortune, and the thrill of discovery. Despite over a century of searching, no one had ever come upon the hidden entrance to Breezeway Cave. That is, until April 1993, when cavers chanced upon an obscure blowing hole revealing its location.

Caver Al Hinman felt behind a boulder next to a game trail paralleling the canyon wall and, to his surprise, a cool breeze encouraged him to linger. Calling his companions over to join him, Hinman asked the others to feel the wind.

Often, air blowing from behind a rock means little. In many cases, the wind is simply a chimney effect, flowing from a higher or lower location through tiny crevices and spaces and emerging at another. In this case, however, the three cavers quickly became convinced there was more to the wind than the surface indicated.

Pulling away dirt and rock from the hole, the three could see signs of solution in the limestone. Just under the surface, a low space was filled nearly to the ceiling with packrat droppings, suggesting animals lived in this breezy opening for many years.

Geologically, the opening was in a prime location for a major cave. Indeed, nearby was a small cave that had been visited for most of the century.

Eagerly excavating their discovery, the cavers quickly were into the first small chamber. Through clouds of billowing dust they dug, passing buckets outside for dumping of debris. In only a few weeks of digging, the new cave, called Breezeway for its prominent breeze, was large enough for two cavers to work inside at a single time.

The cavers pushed deeper into the mountain, following an obvious fracture in the ceiling of the claustrophobic chamber. Eventually, the passage reached a region of large, broken rocks. These were passed out of the cave for disposal.

Ahead was an open, jagged passage. With care, it was possible to find a route through the rocks to enlarging passage beyond. On May 22, 1993, the cavers successfully pushed through the fractured rock into solutional cave passage.

Though not large, the passage provided an opportunity to progress without continued digging. In just a few minutes, the team slid through some tight squeezes and climbed up and into a major new chamber.

Dark and echoing, the new room was named Cowboy Heaven. As large as any room in the Cave of the Winds, it led deeper into the mountain. Down a short pit called the Hangman's Hole, through a forest of columns and stalactites called the Jailbars, the cavers entered a high canyon they named Happy Trails. Briefly investigating this new find, the team headed back for the surface, excited at the prospect of another major cave for Williams Canyon.

In the weeks that followed, a growing number of cavers were invited to participate in the exploration and survey of Breezeway Cave. Under an oath of secrecy, the cavers explored and charted thousands of feet of passageway, much of it beautifully decorated. A high climb led up to a pool basin called Holy Waters, where for several years cavers were required to remove their muddy boots, gloves, and coveralls to traverse a narrow ledge providing access to the cave beyond. Today, a bridge crosses the pool offering easier access.

Following Holy Waters, the passage enlarged and then

Anthodites like these are exceptionally delicate. Chambers like the Celestial City, Vanity Fair, the Elkhorn Chambers, and Heaven's Gate have many such displays of both anthodites and beaded helictites. (Photo by David Harris.)

dropped into the Celestial City, a chamber filled with delicate beaded helictites, similar to those previously found in the Cave of the Winds. As stunning as these formations are, it was easy to ignore them for another blowing hole was found not far from the entrance to this chamber.

Through the summer and fall of 1993, cavers spent hours excavating the mud-filled passage leading below the wall of the Celestial City. Called the Antelope Freeway, a steady wind encouraged cavers to dig harder to stay warm. Finally, in February 1994, cavers successfully completed their dig, emerging in unknown passageways.

On the far side of the Freeway, the cave opened up. Another chamber of beaded helictites, the Elkhorn Chambers, featured a dazzling display called the Tesla Coil. Named for nineteenth century inventor Nikola Tesla, the basketball-sized group of helictites is larger than anything in the Cave of the Winds. Many consider it the most beautiful beaded helictite group currently known in any cave.

Through a series of squeezes, climbs, and crawls, another helictite chamber astounded the explorers. For twenty-five feet, the wall of Heaven's Gate is filled with white beaded helictites so delicate that one dares not closely approach it. Visitors often quietly sit in wonder of the chamber, thinking perhaps this room is as close to Heaven as they can get on Earth.

More delights and surprises awaited the explorers. After Heaven's Gate, the cave enlarges to tunnels large enough for automobile traffic. A colossal room, Stone River, is reached at the end of one tunnel. It contains several large lakes, a steep mud slope, exquisite formations, and a large river of flowstone. One caver stripped down and swam across a frigid lake to the far side, hoping to find additional passage. The cave, however, did not continue in that direction.

Over the next few months, Breezeway exploration continued at full speed. A team of climbers successfully scaled the precipitous wall of Stone River to enter another large chamber above known as High Plains. Another group pushed through a nasty, twisting belly crawl called the Sidewinder. It led to Rattlesnake Canyon, the Velvet Underground, and several thousand feet of lower-level passage. Within a few months, surveying in Breezeway had reached the mile mark. By 1995, the cave neared seven thousand feet of passage.

Exploration continues to this day in Breezeway, though not at the remarkable rate of the mid 1990s. Publicity about the cave remained remarkably restrained through the decade, excepting a story on Romanian National Television.

A sturdy gating and security system installed by the Cave of the Winds protects Breezeway, the management seeing the cave as an investment for the future. At present, there are no plans on commercializing the cave, in part because of its inaccessibility and delicacy. Williams Canyon Project trips into Breezeway are strictly restricted to work and science-related projects. Even with the restrictions, and the best efforts of cavers, the cave has suffered some degradation, including damaged dripstone and flowstone.

Cave conservationists consider Breezeway to be a work in progress: can cavers take care in their movements underground to protect the cave environment? Or, will the overwhelming interest in the continuing exploration of the cave bring irreversible harm?

Cavers are amazed at the contrast between the clean white anthodites and frostwork with the red muddy clay that is found beneath. For many, the experience is almost mystical. (Photo by David Harris.)

For the cavers who originally discovered and opened Breezeway, the choice is clear—exceptional care must be taken while moving through the cave and every effort must be made to protect it from harm. It is everyone's responsibility to protect and preserve this underground jewel.

*The Crystal Palace. In 1885,
the Cave of the Winds opened a suite
of four chambers collectively called
the Crystal Palace. Filled with
"flowering alabaster," the ceilings of
the rooms delighted visitors.
Unfortunately, the close proximity of
the delicate formations to the visitor
trail doomed them. Some visitors
could not keep their hands away and
the helictites greatly suffered. (Photo
from Cave of the Winds collection.)*

Chapter Five
protecting caves

When man enters the underground world, he enters an extraordinary place. Here, time takes on new meaning, as many caves are secluded from the erosional forces of wind, rain, and ice. Penciled signatures and candle soot marks on the ceiling from visitors a century ago appear as if they were placed yesterday. A handprint in the soft dirt of a floor might last millennia, given the proper circumstances.

The forces of nature can be extraordinary patient in creating these treasured places. Unfortunately, carelessness and greed by thoughtless visitors can instantly damage delicate underground features, bringing eternal harm that will never be repaired within the life of all mankind.

These hidden lands deserve both our respect and protection. Though we can gaze in awe and appreciation of the wondrous sights, we must never touch nor harm these unique features. Care must be taken in traveling through these places, with exceptional awareness of movement.

In the Cave of the Winds, the Crystal Palace once astounded visitors with breathtaking vistas of sparkling white helictites stretching the length of the chamber. Today, this corridor is but a remnant of its former splendor owing to the selfishness of insensitive visitors.

In mourning the loss of the Crystal Palace, let it also serve as a warning for future generations that pass beneath its ravaged length. While its beauty is but a fading memory, there are many more places in the caves of Williams Canyon and elsewhere that offer similar dazzling sights. They deserve the trust of man the Crystal Palace did not receive.

Desperate measures. By the middle part of the twentieth century, the management of the Cave of the Winds resorted to installing chicken wire and stern warning signs in the cave to discourage vandals. Unfortunately, the cave still suffered damage. This view from 1958 is of the Nursery, not far from the Crystal Palace. (Photo from Cave of the Winds collection.)

Wonders Underground. Protection of delicate, rare mineral speleothems like these in Breezeway Cave is a primary concern for all cavers. (Photo by David Harris.)

Chapter Six
additional information
about caves

Individuals interested in learning more about caves and caving are invited to contact the National Speleological Society, the largest and most prestigious national association for caving and speleological studies in the United States. Founded in 1941, the organization has about two hundred chapters called grottos around the country, including several in Colorado. The Williams Canyon Project is an official project of the Society and has worked in the caves of the canyon since 1982.

The Society maintains a comprehensive Internet web site at www.caves.org. The site contains information about the organization and its member chapters. The NSS can also be reached by telephone and mail.

The National Speleological Society
2813 Cave Avenue
Hunstville, Alabama 35810-4431
Telephone: (256) 852-1300

For more information regarding commercial caves in the United States contact the National Caves Association at www.cavern.com.

Cave of the Winds
P.O. Box 826
Manitou Springs, CO 80829
Telephone: (719) 685-5444
www.caveofthewinds.com

Acknowledgments

Over the last two decades, Colorado cavers have been permitted to explore and study the wonderful caves of Williams Canyon, including the Cave of the Winds. For this privilege, our volunteer Williams Canyon Project owes much to the cave's general manager, Grant Carey. Through his support and understanding, our group has learned much about the caves and has made many remarkable discoveries.

Since the mid-1980s, Donald G. Davis has coordinated the historical research of the Cave of the Winds. He and I have spent many hours looking through historical newspapers and microfilm, seeking out forgotten books and arguing the finer points of history. I owe him much for his exceptional efforts.

In the publication of this book, I must thank Barbara Bolton, the Project Director for The Donning Company/Publishers, and Sally Davis, my editor. Thanks also to Paul Burger for drafting a map of the Cave of the Winds.

Of course, much of this book is dependent on the superb photography contained within. Thanks to David Harris for his photographic assistance and to the Cave of the Winds staff for allowing me to select images from the cave's archives.

Finally, thanks to the many National Speleological Society cavers who have participated in trips to the caves of Williams Canyon. Their tireless efforts have helped recognize the potential of the canyon first recognized by cave developer George Snider.

Richard Rhinehart
April 21, 2000

Richard Rhinehart, standing at the collapsed entrance to the Manitou Grand Cavern, 2000. (Photo by David Harris.)

about the author

A noted cave explorer and historian on Colorado caving history, Richard Rhinehart is the founding editor of Colorado's prestigious caving journal *Rocky Mountain Caving*. A journalism graduate of the University of Colorado with published articles on caves in the *National Speleological Society News*, *American Caves* from the American Cave Conservation Association, the Denver Museum of Natural History's *Bear Pause* and Denver's *Rocky Mountain Sports*; Rhinehart has actively explored and studied Colorado caves since 1974. He is a recognized Fellow of the National Speleological Society and a founding director of the Society's Williams Canyon Project. Rhinehart is a past representative of the Colorado Cave Survey and a member of two local Society chapters. He makes his home in Colorado Springs.